Полюби голубку (горлинку)

by

Bradley Zink

Translated by: Valery Pakhomov

DEDICATION

To my parents, Jon and Stephanie, for teaching me how to be a man, to my wife, Natasha, for helping to make me the man I am today, and to my son, Alex, for giving me the desire to become the man I should be.

ACKNOWLEDGMENTS

I would like to thank all the hard work and devotion that goes into the conservation efforts. With the ongoing efforts, and support of organizations like the San Diego Zoo and Safari Park, the public is able to enjoy the beauty of these amazing animals.

And a special thank you to my friend, and father-in-law, Valery Pakhomov, for translating my book into Russian. This is all you!

Contents

Mourning Dove

Полюби голубку (горлинку)

Meerkat

Присядь поговорить с мангустом

African Lion

Не ссорься с большим котом

Waller's Gazelle (Gerenuk)

Будь гордый как газель

Southern White Rhino

Посмотри обед носорога

Lorikeet

Будь ласковым к попугайчику

Ring-tailed Lemur

Восхищайся лемуром

African Elephant

Уважай слона

African Spoonbill

Порадуйся цапле

Eastern Giant Eland

Подружись с антилоп**ой**

Blue Macaw

Восхищайся попугаем

Rothschild Giraffe

Посмейся с жирафом

Chilean Flamingo

Посочуствуй фламинго

Gemsbok

Остановись поговорить с ориксом

Sable Antelope

Обнадёжь антилопу

Wildebeest

Раздели пиршество с антилопой-гну

Rodrigues Fruit Bat

<u>Ч</u>то это   Спящая летучая мышь

Goat

Подурачся с козлом

Victoria Crowned Pigeon

Поудивляйся   с голубем

Orangutan

СТАНЬ ПОКЛОННИКОМ ОРАНГУТАНА

ABOUT THE AUTHOR

Born in Petaluma, California during the early 1970's, Bradley Zink grew up with a passion for books. Instilled in him by his parents, and surrounded with a library of books by Dr. Seuss, Mark Twain and Charles Dickens, to name a few, he developed a true passion for reading.

After the birth of his son, Alex, and being a stay-at-home dad, he too instilled the power of reading in his son, too. Using Dr. Seuss as the building blocks for teaching him, Bradley aspired to create a book for Alex, and all children to enjoy. With his son as his muse and inspiration, Bradley is constantly testing out his writings on the world's harshest critic, his son Alex.